Chil
B.
a division of Hodd

D1424975

Produced by Fowke & Co. for Hodder Children's Books

Cover photo: supplied by Hulton Archive. 'Bombed Out' reference HP5483.

Published by Hodder Children's Books 2002

0 340 85183 X

10 9 8 7 6 5 4 3 2 1

Hodder Children's Books
a division of Hodder Headline Limited
338 Euston Road
London NW1 3BH

Printed and bound by the Guernsey Press Co. Ltd., Channel Islands
A Catalogue record for this book is available from the British Library

CONTENTS

 Watch out for the *Sign of the Foot*! Whenever you see this sign in the book it means there are some more details at the *FOOT* of the page. Like here.

BLAST OFF!

BACKGROUND TO THE BLITZ

QUESTIONS AND ANSWERS

Question: what goes into a house?
Answer: a life.

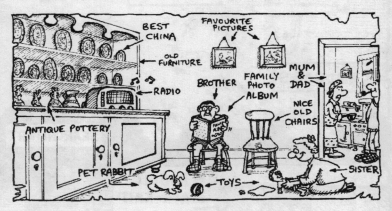

Question: how long does it take to destroy a house?
Answer: no time at all. A large *sprengbombe*, such as those dropped from German Dornier and Heinkel bombers in World War II, can smash a house into a pile of rubble in a few seconds.

 Means 'high explosive bomb'.

Blast it!

'Blitz ' is the name given to the German bombing campaign against Britain during World War II. At the height of the Blitz, bombs fell not in ones and twos but in *thousands*. 27,500 tons of high explosive were

BRITISH FIGHTERS

SANDBAGS

SEARCHLIGHT

PUBLIC AIR-RAID SHELTER

AIR RAID PRECAUTIONS WARDEN (ARP)

Blitz comes from *Blitzkrieg* meaning 'lightning war'. *Blitzkrieg* was the German name for their tactic of striking very hard and fast at the start of World War II, using tanks, soldiers and planes together.

dropped on Britain, mainly on London, thousands of lives were lost and tens of thousands of houses were destroyed. It's hard for us now to imagine what life was like for those who lived and worked in London and other big cities during that terrible time.

ACK-ACK FIRE

GERMAN BOMBERS

BARRAGE BALLOONS

AUXILIARY FIRE SERVICE (AFS)

ANTI-AIRCRAFT (ACK-ACK) GUNS IN A PILLBOX

TRAINED RESCUE WORKERS

BATH BOMBS

During the course of World War II, 60,595 British people were killed by German bombers and even more Germans were killed by British and American bombers. At the peak of the Blitz, between August 1940 and May 1941, air raids on London were almost non-stop. On top of those killed, over 100,000 people were seriously injured.

Bomb blast itself was a strange thing. It might shave off the front of a building and expose someone sitting in their bath, completely safe if a little embarrassed. Or it might knock down all the houses in a street leaving just one standing in the middle. You never knew when your turn might come. People learned to live with the uncertainty. In fact for many of them, it added a little spice to their lives.

Incredibly brave volunteer firemen and air raid wardens fought the flames and tried to rescue the victims from the rubble. And somehow people carried on with their lives while the Blitz was raging. After each raid they dusted themselves off and went back to work or play as before. Phones were mended, broken glass was swept away and buses were kept running as best they could be.

SEALION WHAT I MEAN?

When the first bombs fell on London in August 1940, Britain and Germany had already been at war for eleven months. During those eleven months the powerful German war machine had conquered Norway, Holland, Belgium and France. Now it was ready to invade Britain, codename *Operation Sealion*.

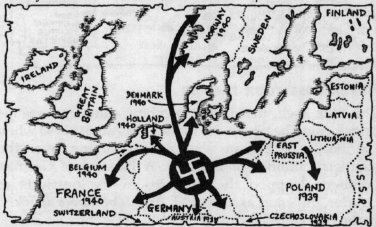

Being an island, Britain had one important advantage over the rest of Germany's victims. In order to conquer it, the German army would have to be shipped across the English Channel in the face of fierce opposition from Britain's navy and air force. The German invasion fleet might be sunk before it could reach

British shores or might be utterly destroyed while trying to land. It was vital for Germany to destroy the RAF before the planned invasion. German attempts to destroy the RAF and the RAF's stubborn resistance are known as the *Battle of Britain*, the only major battle ever to have been fought entirely in the air.

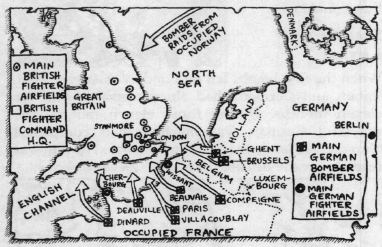

NEVER LOSE YOUR TEMPER

The Blitz itself, that is, the bombing campaign against British cities, began on the night of 24 August 1940 when the Battle of Britain was already raging over the southern counties of England. A handful of German bombers dropped their bombs on the outskirts of London - and as a reprisal, British bombers attacked Berlin, the German capital.

Hermann Goering, the leader of the *Luftwaffe*, the German air force, was furious that the British air force

---

Actually this was a mistake by the German pilots who were under orders *not* to bomb non-military targets at this time, although there was no way that the British could know that it was a mistake.

had managed to slip past his defences and attack Berlin. It made him look foolish. On 3 September, egged on by a phone call from Adolf Hitler, the German leader, he called a conference of his commanders and ordered them to attack British cities.

A few days later, Keith Park, head of RAF Fighter Command looked down on the East End of London, blackened and burning after a massive German raid, and said:

Which may well seem a strange thing to say. However it was at that moment that Park realised that Germany was going to *lose* the Battle of Britain. By switching their attack onto British cities, the Germans as good as *stopped* attacking the Royal Air Force - and it was the RAF which should have been their main target. They had given the RAF a precious breathing space for the fight back.

BLAST IN THE BATH!

These dishevelled ducks have got separated from their dates due to bomb blast. Can you put them back together again?

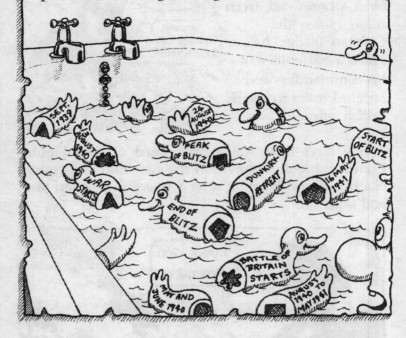

JERRY BUILDING

AN ANGRY NATION FIGHTS BACK

JERRY GROWS UP

'Jerry' was what British soldiers called German soldiers during World War II. The Germans called the British soldiers 'Tommy'.

1920s: Times were tough in Europe in the 1920s, especially in Germany where the *deutschmark*, the German currency, plummeted in value, creating a major economic crisis.

This meant that the Germans had to pay more and more for everything. A cup of coffee could double in price between sips. Wages had to increase to keep in step but never quite did so - people spent their wages as soon as they got them, or else they went hungry.

1930: The start of the 1930s were no better, at least not to start with. Many workers lost their jobs and their families went hungry. That's why the decade is often called the 'hungry thirties'.

1933: In 1933 the Germans voted a new political party into power, hoping it would sort out their problems. The leader of the *National German Workers' Party* (Nazis for short) was a failed Austrian artist and World War I sergeant called Adolf Hitler.

1934: Hitler started to build up Germany's armed forces. Soon German factories were churning out guns, tanks, planes and ammunition. This meant that there was now work for everyone.

Suddenly Germany was booming - which meant that the Nazis became even more popular.

1936: Once he felt strong enough, Hitler used his armed forces to get what he wanted. He believed that the Germans needed *lebensraum* - living space. In 1936, his troops occupied the Sudetenland in southern Germany, forbidden to them by the peace treaty signed at the end of World War I. In 1938 he took over Austria and in March 1939 he invaded Czechoslovakia. It seemed that nothing could stop him.

1939: Finally, in September 1939, the Germans invaded Poland. This time Hitler really had gone too far. Britain and France realised that they had to do something to stop him. On 3 September, they declared war on Germany.

Not that the Germans took a blind bit of notice. They went ahead and carved up Poland between themselves and the Russians.

1939: The British army took up positions in France and Holland to await the expected German attack.

1939-40: The British soldiers waited - and waited - and waited. This period is called the 'phoney war' because, although war had been declared, no one did any fighting.

May 1940: In May 1940, the German war machine smashed through Denmark and invaded Norway. It was too easy.

The British and French tried to help the Norwegians but their help was too little and came too late.

May 1940: After Germany invaded Norway, the British people decided that they were fed up with their government which seemed to have done nothing to stop Hitler and his Nazis, despite having declared war on them.

To howls of 'Go! Go! Go!', even from members of his own Conservative party, the British Prime Minister Neville Chamberlain resigned.

Neville Chamberlain was replaced by Winston Churchill on 10 May 1940. The new Prime Minister was determined to fight back.

WE'VE LOST SO MUCH TIME... WE'RE UNPREPARED FOR THE BATTLE TO COME! BUT WE WILL PREVAIL!

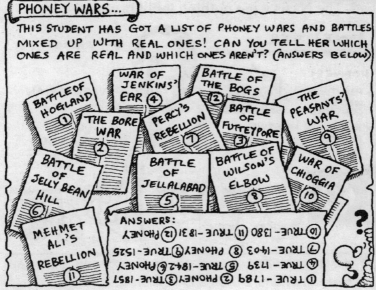

PHONEY WARS...

THIS STUDENT HAS GOT A LIST OF PHONEY WARS AND BATTLES MIXED UP WITH REAL ONES! CAN YOU TELL HER WHICH ONES ARE REAL AND WHICH ONES AREN'T? (ANSWERS BELOW)

BATTLE OF HOGLAND ①

WAR OF JENKINS' EAR ④

BATTLE OF THE BOGS ⑫

THE BORE WAR ②

PERCY'S REBELLION ⑦

BATTLE OF FUTTEYPORE ③

THE PEASANTS' WAR ⑨

BATTLE OF JELLY BEAN HILL ⑥

BATTLE OF JELLALABAD ⑤

BATTLE OF WILSON'S ELBOW ⑧

WAR OF CHIOGGIA ⑩

MEHMET ALI'S REBELLION ⑪

ANSWERS:
① TRUE - 1789 ② PHONEY ③ TRUE - 1857
④ TRUE - 1739 ⑤ TRUE - 1842 ⑥ PHONEY
⑦ TRUE - 1403 ⑧ PHONEY ⑨ TRUE - 1525
⑩ TRUE - 1380 ⑪ TRUE - 1831 ⑫ PHONEY

SPOT THE MONSTER

ADOLF

Adolf Hitler (1889-1945) was born Adolf Schicklgruber, the son of an Austrian customs official. When still a young man, having failed as an artist in Vienna, he moved to Germany and fought in World War I (1914-18). In 1919 he became the seventh member of a tiny, new political party - the Nazi Party and soon he was its leader. He was a racist who believed that Germans were members of a 'master race' called Aryans 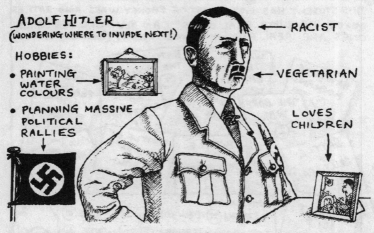. Under his leadership, Germany would build an empire which would last for a thousand years, the *Thousand Year Reich* as it's known.

Meanwhile Germany would cleanse itself of what Hitler thought of as 'lesser' people living within its borders such as Jews, gypsies and people with disabilities. And if that meant killing them - well, too bad. The Nazis were nothing if not brutal.

ADOLF HITLER
(WONDERING WHERE TO INVADE NEXT!)

HOBBIES:
- PAINTING WATER COLOURS
- PLANNING MASSIVE POLITICAL RALLIES

← RACIST

← VEGETARIAN

LOVES CHILDREN

Aryan included other north Europeans such as Scandinavians, Dutch and British.

WINSTON

Winston Churchill (1874-1965), Winnie for short, liked to live well and was famous for his eccentricity. He once greeted the American President Theodore Roosevelt when standing naked in the bath. He said:

The Prime Minister of Britain has nothing to hide from the President of the United States.

Churchill began his career as a soldier in 1895, then took up journalism and became a superb writer. He entered Parliament in 1900 and by 1940 he was a very senior politician. When Winnie took over in 1940, he electrified the country in a series of brilliant speeches.

We shall fight with growing confidence and growing strength in the air, we shall defend our island whatever the cost may be. We shall fight on the beaches, we shall fight on the landing grounds ... we shall never surrender .

WINSTON CHURCHILL
(SPEAKING TO THE NATION IN HIS FAMOUS 'SIREN SUIT')

LIKES AN AFTERNOON NAP, BIG CIGARS, CHAMPAGNE AND BRANDY

BBC

HOBBIES: PAINTING AND BRICKLAYING

GREAT SPEECHWRITER

PATRIOTIC

Speech given in Parliament 4 June 1940.

A NARROW ESCAPE

Winnie was ready for war but
Britain and France weren't. The
German armies smashed through
Holland and invaded France, using
their favourite tactic of *Blitzkrieg*.
The French and British armies were
no match for them.

The British and some of their French allies  were forced
back into a narrow strip of land around the French port
of Dunkirk.

Dunkirk was where the
British had their first lucky
break. The Germans could
probably have forced the
British army into the sea.
The British were completely
outgunned. But Hermann
Goering, the leader of the
Luftwaffe, persuaded Hitler
that the *Luftwaffe* could
defeat the British on its own
and that there was no need
to risk German tanks and
soldiers in the battle.

 Allies are nations which have agreed to come to each other's assistance
if attacked.

20

When Goering's *Luftwaffe* attacked the British army at Dunkirk, it was the first time that German planes came up against RAF planes flying direct from their bases in England. Shortage of fuel meant that the British fighters only had fifteen minutes of fighting time over Dunkirk, but, added together, all those fifteen minutes were enough to give the Germans a rude shock.

Between 27 May and 4 June, 228,000 British soldiers and 110,000 French soldiers escaped from Dunkirk back to Britain in a fleet of ships of all shapes and sizes, despite the best efforts of the *Luftwaffe* to stop them.

By the time the evacuation from Dunkirk was complete, the RAF had lost 509 fighter planes in the fighting over Europe and 435 pilots had been lost, killed or captured. It still had a few cards up its sleeve, but not many ...

HERMANN THE GERMAN

During World War I, Hermann Goering joined the German air force and became an 'ace' fighter pilot. When it was over he joined the Nazi Party (1922, three years after Hitler). He usually agreed with Hitler's decisions slavishly, which Hitler liked. Goering was rewarded with top jobs. By the time the war had started Hitler had made him: Air Minister, Commander-in-chief of the German Air Force, Head of the Nazi four-year economic plan, President of the Prussian Council and President of the Reichstag ☜. After the war, when asked what Goering was like, a German officer replied:

He was like your Henry VIII, but Henry had the wives and Goering had the jobs.

Goering loved luxury. He would sometimes meet his guests clothed in a purple dressing gown smelling of perfume and with rouge on his cheeks. Then he would show them his collection of paintings, looted from the art galleries of Europe. His personal train, code name 'Asia', had a cinema and compartments for his valet, his cook - and his nurse. He was always overweight and he took drugs given to him by his personal doctor. Those drugs were worth a fleet of fighters to the British during the war. It was probably drug addiction which caused him to make his worst decisions, of which there were plenty.

The *Reichstag* was the German parliament.

SEALIONS AGAIN

After Dunkirk the German army controlled all the European coastline opposite Britain. It was time to make plans for invasion - codename, Operation *Seelöwe* or Sealion. This was no easy matter, even for the victorious German war machine. An opposed landing on an enemy shore is probably the most difficult of all military manoeuvres. It would have to be massive: 3,000 barges and 155 transport ships would be needed. The top German generals were anxious. In a set of orders of 2 July, the Chiefs of Staff of the German army stated:

A landing in England is possible - provided air superiority can be obtained.

In other words: it was up to Goering. High on drugs, he prophesied that the RAF's defence of Britain would last four or five days at most. And in a fit of decisiveness, he ordered his luxury train to Beauvais in France - although he continued to stay with his wife in his luxury mansion back in Germany.

DON'T FORGET YOUR TOOTHBRUSH

WE'RE READY FOR YOU – WELL, ALMOST

GAS!

Before the war started, the British government had prepared for the worst. A million funeral forms were printed. That was how many they thought might die in a German bombing campaign. A special report suggested that, in addition, four million people might need mental treatment, and gas masks were got ready in vast quantities.

Gas was what they feared most of all. Poison gas had caused terrible suffering to the troops in World War I just twenty years earlier, and when war was declared on 3 September 1939, everyone expected the Germans to drop gas bombs. The British government issued gas masks to all its citizens. Gas masks were horribly uncomfortable. Everyone had to practise putting them on - you put your chin in first and then you spat on the window which was meant to stop it from misting up.

There was a rubber washer under your chin, that flipped up and hit you every time you breathed in ... the bottom of the mask soon filled up with spit, and your face got hot and sweaty.

There were special gas-cots for babies; mum or someone had to pump air in from the side. Some horses even had gas masks.

Young children were issued with coloured gas masks. There was one that looked like Mickey Mouse.

Posh kids carried their masks in special leather boxes. You could tell the poor kids because they had to use the standard canvas case.

TIME TO GO

The Germans were bound to bomb major cities first. That's where the biggest arms factories were, and in any modern war it's very important to stop your enemy's supplies of fresh weapons and ammunition. Before the war started, the government had laid plans for a mass 'evacuation' of city children to safer parts of the country. By December 1939, most London children had left town, the same went for Manchester, Birmingham and the other big cities.

When the time came to leave, each child carried a gas mask plus a bag or brown paper parcel for spare clothes (if they had any). They wore labels with their name and the name and address of their school. Sometimes their mothers went with them but more often they went with other children from their school under the care of a teacher. Most had never been away from home before:

We had one teacher in each compartment in charge of twelve pupils. When the train departed the wailing and tears echoed up and down the train.

On arrival at the town or village where they were to stay, the children were usually taken to the local school or church hall. Then the local people who were to look after them came to choose. It was a bit like a cattle market, people chose the children they thought would be easiest to look after. It was pot luck on both sides. Some children ended up with really kind families - but others weren't so lucky.

ALL SEWN UP

The poverty of many evacuee children came as a shock to most of the middle and upper class families who had to look after them. Some evacuees had never used a knife and fork before, and some evacuees were sewn into their clothes for the winter, like in the Middle Ages:

... you could tell those ones a mile off.

When they reached their new homes the evacuees found everything so strange and new that there was an epidemic of bed-wetting. Many were used to sleeping six or seven in a bed, others had never slept in a bed at all and were used to sleeping on the floor beneath their parents' bed. A bed of their own was a real shock - and lonely.

As for the countryside - well, some children loved it and others never got used to it. A lot of them had never seen a cow before. Here's a description by a London boy:

The head is for the purpose of growing horns and so the mouth can be somewhere. The horns are to butt with, and the mouth is to moo with. Under the cow hangs the milk.

Another child when she saw horses and hens in the same field together asked:

... won't the horses eat the chickens?

REFUGEES

Along with evacuees from the towns, children who were refugees from Nazi-controlled Europe also needed somewhere safe to stay. Often they were the children of Jewish parents who stayed behind and were later murdered by the Nazis. The contrast between Nazi Europe and the English countryside was even greater than the contrast between British cities and the country. The Nazis were so brutal and the English countryside was so peaceful by comparison. Sometimes the locals hardly seemed to care that a country called Germany existed. One teenage refugee from Austria described arriving in Barnstaple in Devon. At tea the locals discussed the undesirable number of foreigners coming to the town. He started to feel uncomfortable then:

I realised ... that these 'foreigners' came from Yorkshire or Lancashire.

The locals weren't bothered about him at all!

EEYUP ME OWD!

GUTEN MORGEN!

HOME AGAIN

The Phoney War dragged on. People said it would all be over by Christmas, although as one little girl remarked:

People kept saying that the war would be over by Christmas - but they didn't say which Christmas.

Summer drifted into winter. The bombs didn't fall. By January nearly half the evacuees had gone home to the cities.

But then in June came Dunkirk, the soldiers arrived back in England, exhausted after their long retreat - and the Germans were on the coast of France. Suddenly war was very real again. Rumour said that the Germans were planning to invade on 15 August.

GERMAN INVASION MAY BE POSTPONED DUE TO LACK OF SIGNPOSTS, SHOCK!

In case of German invasion, all signposts had been taken down when war was declared. This was expected to confuse the invaders. Streets signs were painted out and anti-tank traps were laid across many roads. The traps probably wouldn't have held up the Germans for more than five minutes. As for the lack of signposts - it confused the British as much as it would have confused the Germans.

Meanwhile, German spies were thought to be lurking everywhere. Government posters advised:

A rumour spread that in Holland, German parachutists had disguised themselves as nuns. One of them had been spotted in a railway carriage because his hairy wrists gave him away. In any case, open fields near the coast were planted with poles to stop gliders and parachutists from landing.

DAD'S ARMY

Back in May, a month before Dunkirk, Anthony Eden, the Foreign Secretary, had appealed on the BBC for men who were too old or too young to be regular soldiers to become 'local defence volunteers'. A million men joined by August. This was the start of the Home Guard - 'Dad's Army' as it's become known. There weren't enough rifles to go round because they were needed by the regular army, so the volunteers drilled with shotguns, clubs and even old swords. The Mid-Devon Hunt formed themselves into a troop of cavalry.

How could this army of old men and boys stand up to the Germans? The German newspapers described the Home Guard squads as 'suicide academies'. An Austrian refugee, who had watched Nazi thugs strutting through the streets of Vienna, wondered how the British could be so ignorant of what they were up against. But then he changed his mind:

In the evening the local defence volunteers came out with shotguns and pikes, would you believe it? People who do this cannot lose, they never know when they've lost.

It might have been wishful thinking, but as Hitler was about to find out - it wasn't.

DOGFIGHT!

Bombers beaten in Battle of Britain

The eagle has almost taken off

The job of the *Luftwaffe* was to smash British defences before the planned invasion. The job of the RAF was to stop them. Goering set the date for his big air attack - 13 August 1940, code name *Adlertag*, meaning 'Eagle Day'.

Having set the date, Goering prepared his forces - well, actually he spent most of July in his luxury house in Germany or sight-seeing with his wife in recently-conquered Paris. The *Luftwaffe* high command prepared his forces without him. By 12 August, over a thousand German bombers and fighters were ready on airfields in Belgium, Holland and northern France.

The evening before Eagle Day, German bombers tried to destroy British radar stations and thus 'blind' the British defences. Next morning the first massed flight of German bombers and their fighter escorts headed across the Channel for England.

The Battle of Britain had begun.

RULES FOR STAYING ALIVE

It was a lovely summer for a battle. From August and into September, day after warm, sunny day, people in the south-east of England strained their necks with staring up into the lovely blue sky which should have been so peaceful, but wasn't. The planes, small as insects, twisted and turned, their engines labouring on the climb and changing pitch on the dive. White

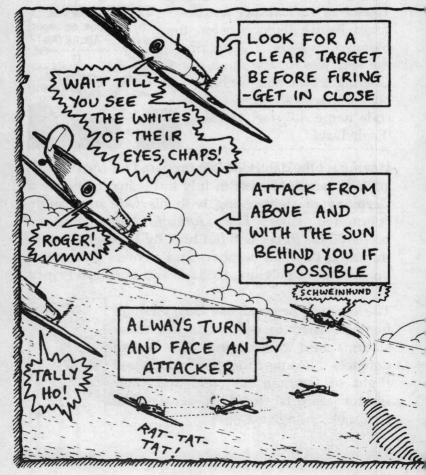

vapour trails traced the movements of their deadly dance for the watchers below, who could just hear the remote sputter of the machine guns.

For the pilots there was no time to stop and stare. Death came quickly to those who made mistakes. The rules of aerial combat hadn't changed very much since World War I.

A GOOD DRESSING DOWN

As the weeks passed the British pilots, who were mostly very young men, bothered less and less about regulations. It was partly a matter of style: the British didn't *want* to look too military like the Germans did. Some pilots flew in their shirt sleeves if the weather was very warm, and some liked to fly with their cockpits open because they could see better.

And it was partly a matter of convenience. As the battle rose to a peak in September, pilots had to fly missions almost round the clock. They slept in their clothes, ready to take off at a moment's notice. They were so tired they 'needed match sticks to prop their eyelids open'. No one was going to bother too much about tidy uniforms at a time like that.

MY DAY, BY AN ACE

4.30am. Woken by airman orderly, quickly put on flying kit.

4.40am. Check that plane is prepared for immediate 'scramble' (take-off).

5.00am. Return to dispersal hut for cup of acorn coffee . Fall asleep in chair.

5.30am. Order to scramble: 'fifty demons approaching from south-east'.

6.30am. Swoop from the sun. Fierce dogfight follows.

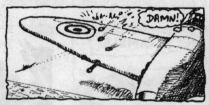

11.30am. Take hit on right wing but manage to keep control of plane.

1.00pm. Return to airfield and land plane safely for refuelling and repairs.

2.00pm. Fall asleep in chair in dispersal hut.

Coffee was a very rare luxury during the war. Acorn coffee made from roasted and ground-up acorns was one alternative.

5.00pm. Order to scramble: 'eighty bandits approaching from south-east'.

5.10pm. Bandits almost on us as we emergency scramble. Fierce dogfight over the airfield, two of ours shot down.

7.10pm. Ordered to intercept large raid approaching southern outskirts of London.

7.30pm. Confused dogfight, many planes involved - and many casualties.

11.00pm. Return to airfield, go to sleep in flying kit - too tired to care.

HUGH DOWDING

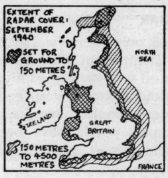

Britain had fewer aircraft than the Germans and fewer pilots. But it *didn't* have Hermann Goering and it *did* have Hugh 'Stuffy' Dowding, the chief of RAF Fighter Command.

Dowding was a dry old stick, thus the nickname 'Stuffy', but very clever. He was one of the few people in Britain who understood how the RAF would have to fight its war against the *Luftwaffe*. He understood that the RAF wasn't strong enough to win; his plan was - *not to lose*. The RAF would defend Britain and stay in the fight. By

not losing to the Germans, the RAF would stop the invasion because the Germans couldn't risk invading while British fighters still flew - so Britain would have won after all.

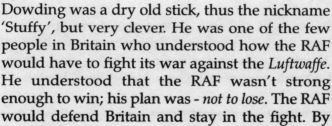

EXTENT OF RADAR COVER: SEPTEMBER 1940

SET FOR GROUND TO 150 METRES

NORTH SEA

IRELAND

GREAT BRITAIN

150 METRES TO 4500 METRES

FRANCE

Thanks to Dowding, when the war started, the south and east coasts of England were ringed by a network of the latest radar masts and the RAF was equipped with modern Spitfire and Hurricane fighters. Dowding had had a tough time preparing for the battle. During the Dunkirk crisis and before, other commanders, including Winston Churchill had demanded that he send more planes to support the army in Europe, but Dowding and Keith Park, commander of the British front line fighters, had held back as many as possible. Thanks to Dowding and Park, when Eagle Day came, the RAF still had just enough planes to defend Britain.

Being right doesn't always make you popular. Even while the Battle of Britain was at its height, Dowding was under notice to retire, and when the battle was over he was forced from his job.

RADAR

It took only *five minutes* for a German bomber to cross the Channel but *fifteen minutes* for a British fighter to take off and then to gain enough height to attack it. Without radar to warn and guide them, the British fighters would have had no chance at all. The Germans would have been able to bomb British airfields almost before the British could take off.

As it was, every time the massed formations of German bombers with their fighter escorts crossed the Channel, a formation of pesky British fighters, forewarned by radar, was waiting to meet them. This baffled the Germans. The sky is huge. How could the British possibly know where to wait?

Radar was the British secret weapon. The Germans had it too but the British put it to better use. It was a question of organisation.

THE TIZZY ANGLE

At the first sign of a blip on the radar screen, the radar operator reported back her best guess of the enemy's line of flight.

Based on this, girls in the Fighter Group operations rooms scattered around the country moved coloured counters on plotting tables. The counters represented planes. By looking at the table one could see at a glance how the battle was progressing.

Using a quick calculation known as the 'Tizzy Angle', after its inventor Sir Henry Tizard, it was then easy to work out the quickest route for British fighters to fly to meet the incoming German bombers.

The British commanders could then direct and redirect their planes to exactly where they were most needed, using radio telegraphy.

SPIT

During the Battle of Britain, just to be cheeky, the German fighter ace Adolf Galland once asked Goering for a squadron of British Spitfires! No wonder - it was a superb plane.

The name was another matter. When Reginald Mitchell, the designer, was told what the RAF intended to call his plane, he said:

Just the sort of bloody silly name they would choose.

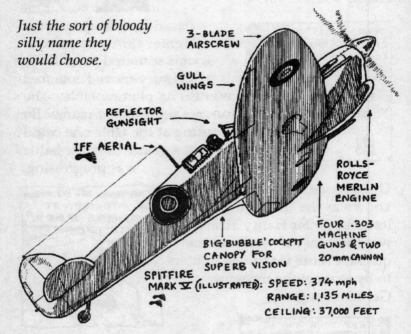

3-BLADE AIRSCREW

GULL WINGS

REFLECTOR GUNSIGHT

IFF AERIAL

ROLLS-ROYCE MERLIN ENGINE

FOUR .303 MACHINE GUNS & TWO 20mm CANNON

BIG 'BUBBLE' COCKPIT CANOPY FOR SUPERB VISION

SPITFIRE MARK V (ILLUSTRATED): SPEED: 374 mph
RANGE: 1,135 MILES
CEILING: 37,000 FEET

Pilots loved flying Spitfires. The 'gull' wings were very thin for high speeds but very strong and gave

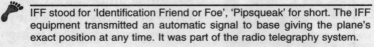

IFF stood for 'Identification Friend or Foe', 'Pipsqueak' for short. The IFF equipment transmitted an automatic signal to base giving the plane's exact position at any time. It was part of the radio telegraphy system.

There were twenty-four different marks of Spitfire from 1936-47. The plane and its armaments changed quite a lot during that time.

maximum lift. Most importantly for the pilots, the wings allowed the Spitfire to turn in a very tight circle. Fighter planes fire from the front. If you're a fighter and you're attacked from behind it's vital to be able to turn sharply so that you can either face your enemy or come up behind him. Who turns tightest often wins.

AND WIND

Actually, the RAF flew many more Hurricanes than Spitfires during the Battle of Britain, and Hurricanes shot down more than half of all German planes shot down by the RAF in the battle. They were quick to make and repair but also excellent to fly. Early models were constructed of wood and fabric over a metal frame. Because of the way they were built, Hurricanes could stand up to exploding shells better than Spitfires although they weren't quite so fast and were not so easy to turn in flight.

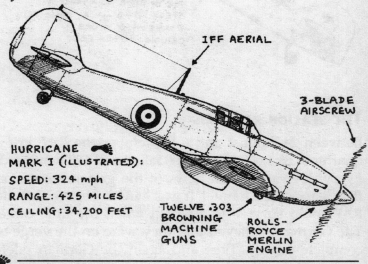

IFF AERIAL

3-BLADE AIRSCREW

HURRICANE
MARK I (ILLUSTRATED):
SPEED: 324 mph
RANGE: 425 MILES
CEILING: 34,200 FEET

TWELVE .303
BROWNING
MACHINE
GUNS

ROLLS-
ROYCE
MERLIN
ENGINE

There were twelve marks of Hurricane from 1935, so the plane changed quite a lot during the war.

Emil

German fighter planes were also very well designed. The best of them during the Battle of Britain was the Messerschmitt Bf 109 E, or 'Emil' as the pilots called it. It was a more delicate plane than the Hurricanes and Spitfires but still a very good plane to fly.

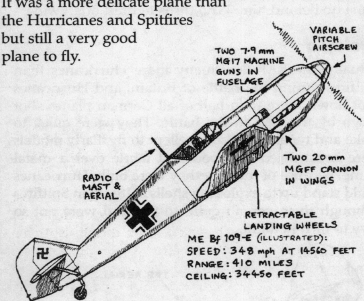

VARIABLE PITCH AIRSCREW

TWO 7·9 mm MG17 MACHINE GUNS IN FUSELAGE

TWO 20 mm MGFF CANNON IN WINGS

RADIO MAST & AERIAL

RETRACTABLE LANDING WHEELS

ME Bf 109-E (ILLUSTRATED):
SPEED: 348 mph AT 14560 FEET
RANGE: 410 MILES
CEILING: 34450 FEET

The sealion retreats

Between 24 August and 6 September the RAF lost a quarter of its 1,000 pilots - 100 killed and 128 wounded. Every day came fresh news of the growing invasion fleet across the Channel. It was hard to believe that the RAF could survive to attack it when the time came. The Germans believed that they were on the verge of complete victory. Time and again the German pilots were told that the British were down to their last fifty fighters, but somehow Dowding always had a few more fighters up his sleeve. The Germans even had a joke about it:

On 15 September, the Germans launched their most massive attack of the battle. This attack was meant to be the final blow which would wipe the British from the skies for good. Wave after wave of bombers supported by fighters crossed the Channel to pound British airfields and factories. Unfortunately for the Germans, those British factories had been working night and day since August to build fresh aircraft and by 15 September the RAF had started to grow stronger. It now had 1,500 pilots and the planes for them to fly. The new Spitfires and Hurricanes tore into the massed ranks of German bombers and the Germans were forced to retreat, losing many more aircraft than the RAF in the process.

Two days later, British intelligence overheard a coded German radio message: Operation Sealion had been put off - on Hitler's order. 15 September 1940, the day that the RAF finally 'didn't lose', is now remembered as 'Battle of Britain Day'.

In the words of Winston Churchill:

Never in the field of human conflict was so much owed by so many to so few .

BLITZ!

BOMBS AND BOMBERS

BLASTING THE BLITZ

13 August 1940: Eagle Day, start of the Battle of Britain. German attacks aimed at airfields and aircraft factories, plus British naval defences.

MUM! IT'S STARTED! THEY'VE BOMBED THE GROCER'S!

OH, NO! IT'S TIME TO PACK HER SUITCASE!

24 August 1940: a handful of German bombers fleeing back to Britain having failed to reach their targets, drop their bombs on the outskirts of London. This leads to the British revenge attack on Berlin and then the German decision to mount revenge attacks on London - and to the start of the Blitz.

7 September 1940: at around 4 o'clock in the afternoon, a massive formation of German bombers and their fighter escorts covering an area 1.5 miles high and 800 square miles of sky is spotted over the Channel, the first major attack on London, aimed at the London docks. Huge fires destroy many buildings.

15 September 1940: the climax of the Battle of Britain. The Germans launch a massive attack but get the worst of it. Operation Sealion is put off.

5 October 1940: the last daylight attack on Britain.

12 October 1940: Night attacks continue on major British cities.

Mid-November 1940: German pilots start deliberate terror bombing of British cities.

10 May 1941: last attack of the Blitz on London, and the heaviest raid of all. A moonlit night and a low tide help the attackers. Firemen are unable to draw enough water from the river Thames to quench the flames.

16 May 1941: the Blitz is finally over.

TARGET PRACTICE

There are two things bombers try to avoid.

1. Getting shot down by the defenders.
2. Wasting their bombs on the wrong targets.

On daylight raids it was easy enough for the German bombers to see where they were going and, until November 1940, the pilots had orders not to drop their bombs unless they could be fairly certain of hitting their targets. But daylight raids grew riskier as the British grew stronger especially after 15 September. Which was why the Germans switched to more night bombing, which was safer but less accurate.

ACH! THERE IS THE THAMES! WE WILL SOON BE OVER THE TARGET!

Moonlit nights were best for the bombers - and worst for their victims. On moonlit nights pilots could follow the course of the silvery River Thames to London or follow the glint of railway lines to the main stations. On such nights, Londoners talked of a 'bombers' moon'.

On dark nights or in bad weather the Germans had to rely on their *Knickebein* radio system, which was simple but effective. Two radio beams were transmitted from sites on the continent. The pilot flew along one beam, until he came to the point where it crossed the other beam. That was the sign that he was near his target. Later they developed the *X-Gerät* system where several side beams cut across the main beam, letting the pilot know how far he had travelled. It was a raid using *X-Gerät* which destroyed Coventry Cathedral one terrible night in 1941. Of course, the British tried to upset the German radio system. They transmitted false radio beacons, 'meacons', to confuse the German pilots. Meacons were part of the 'wizard war', as Churchill called it - scientists on both sides trying to keep one step ahead of each other.

When they arrived at the target area, German advance planes would drop fire bombs as markers for the main wave of bombers. To help the main wave, 'chandeliers', very bright magnesium flares, were floated down on parachutes to light the ground below.

Knickebein means literally 'crooked leg'.

Meanwhile the British might have set off 'starfish' decoy fires to fool the bombers into dropping their bombs elsewhere.

NIGHT FIGHTERS

There's an awful lot of sky over London and other major cities. A bomber is very small by comparison and very hard to shoot down. The best defenders were the British night fighters, painted black. But night fighting was never easy - and it wasn't comfortable. At night in winter the sky was bitterly cold. Pilots wore flying suits, boots and thick gloves to keep warm. Unfortunately, the cockpit of the Hurricane was too small and packed with instruments to allow space for wearing a lot of bulky, warm clothes, so the pilots of Hurricanes tended to freeze.

Government scientists invented an extra-warm boot for them. You poured a special chemical into the empty sole, and when water was added through a little hole, the chemical gave off heat.

GERMAN BOMB PARADE

The Germans dropped a whole range of bombs on Britain, each designed to cause death and destruction in its own special way. Goering favoured bombs with whistles attached so that they made a horrible screaming sound as they came down, which the British called 'screaming meanies'.

Sprengbomben
- high explosive.

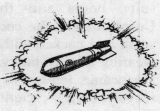

Minenbomben - mines. Landmines were dropped by parachute. They drifted down and were impossible to aim. Their only purpose was to harm civilians and the German pilots were ashamed of them.

Flammenbomben - flame bombs, filled with oil, and phosphorus or magnesium in a rubber solution so that they stuck.

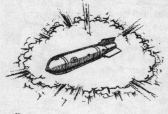

Brandbomben - firebombs, often packed 36 at a time, scattering on impact.

Civilians are people who are not members of a country's armed forces.

GERMAN BOMBERS PARADE

The *Stuka* or *Junkers Ju 87*, was a dive bomber. It had whistles in its wings to make it sound more terrifying and it could dive out of the sky almost vertically before releasing its bombs. The Stuka was useful in Blitzkrieg attacks against soldiers on the ground, but next to hopeless when faced by British defences during the Battle of Britain.

Junkers Ju 88. A high speed bomber and one of the most successful.

Professor Hugo Junkers, who designed the Stuka and the Ju 88, loathed the Nazis. Before the war started, he was arrested and forced to give his company to the German government.

The *Dornier Do 17*, or 'Flying Pencil', was strong and reliable but slow. About a quarter of all German bombers during the Blitz were Dorniers.

The *Heinkel He 111* could carry twice as many bombs as the Dornier, but was also slow.

BARBAROSSA

Barbarossa was the German code name for their planned invasion of Russia. Planning had begun back in July 1940 when the Germans had expected to polish Britain off quickly before attacking their giant neighbour to the east. The poor Russians had no idea that they were about to be attacked - Germany and Russia were allies at the time. The reason that the Blitz stopped in May 1941 was partly because the *Luftwaffe* had failed to destroy the RAF and partly because the Germans needed to move most of their aircraft to the east in readiness for Operation Barbarossa.

BLACKOUTS AND BOMB SHELTERS

LIFE UNDERNEATH

LIGHTS OUT!

Nowadays at night, when seen from the air, Britain is lit up like a jewellery store. Light pollution is overwhelming and in the centre of our towns we can hardly see the stars. The Britain which the German bombers looked down on was completely different, a dark carpet of sleeping fields and buildings, so dark that, looking up, you could see stars even if you were standing in the centre of London. No lights were allowed because they might give clues to the bombers, which were invisible in the dark sky above apart from the drone of their engines.

AND THEN LOOK ACROSS TO THAT SLIGHTLY BRIGHTER ONE AND JOIN THEM UP – LIKE DOT-TO-DOT, ETHEL!

I'M SORRY, HENRY! IT STILL DOESN'T LOOK LIKE A BEAR TO ME!

MORE LIKE A SAUCEPAN IF YOU ASK ME!

Car headlamps were covered over with cardboard or old socks. Unfortunately although this may have helped to fool the bombers, it was dangerous. After 4,000 people had been killed in road accidents, a narrow slit in the cardboard covering was allowed. You could just pick your way by the sliver of light. Dashboard lights were also forbidden. You judged your speed from the sound of the engine.

All windows were screened with black-out curtains.

Torches were covered with tissue paper.

Bus and train windows were covered. Inside they were dark and gloomy. It was easy for cheats to give the conductor the wrong change.

Traffic lights were hooded and covered so that only small crosses of light were allowed to show.

On the up side, at least, there was 'summertime' all year round and 'double summer time' in summer, when it stayed light almost till midnight. In other words, clocks weren't put back an hour at the beginning of winter, instead they were put forward an extra hour in the spring.

BLACKOUT BAMBOOZLER

HOW WOULD <u>YOU</u> HAVE COPED WITH THE BLACKOUT? YOU HAD TO HAVE ACE NIGHT VISION TO SEE WHAT YOU WERE DOING! BELOW IS A LIST OF THINGS YOU MIGHT HAVE SEEN IN 1940. CAN YOU MATCH EACH ITEM TO ITS BLACKED-OUT SILHOUETTE?..

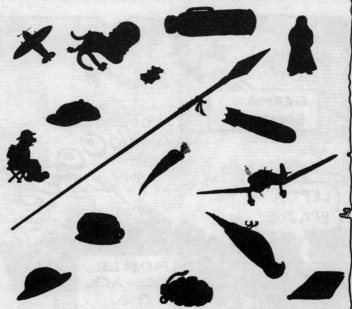

SHRAPNEL • ARP WARDEN • CARROT • BANANA • GRANDAD'S ZULU SPEAR • SPITFIRE • HAND GRENADE • RATION BOOK • CHAMBER POT • GAS MASK • STUKA • DAD'S HOME GUARD HELMET • SCHOOL CAP • NUN • BUDGIE • VACUUM FLASK • UNEXPLODED BOMB •

One item has no silhouette - bananas were very rare in Britain during the war.

It's a Raid Ack-tually

The first warning most people had of a raid was the wail of the air raid sirens, 'banshee howlings' as Churchill described them. Before long everyone was sick and tired of them. Then came the sound of the bombers, a low threatening rumble at first but rising to a deafening roar as they came closer. Then all hell broke lose. Powerful searchlights played across the sky,

and the anti-aircraft or 'ack-ack' guns opened up. On average, 2,000 shells were fired for each plane brought down. It took forty to fifty seconds for a shell to climb to the height of the bombers, so the gunners had to aim in front of the line of flight, which made hitting the bomber almost impossible. Usually, the guns around a city simply shot upwards blind, hoping for a chance hit. That way, at least they made people feel better and they forced the bombers to fly high.

AND THE BALLOON WENT UP

As the war went on and more and more men went off to fight, women took over much of the ground defences. There was an all-woman searchlight regiment and women did everything bar pull the trigger on the guns. They were reckoned to be better operators of the big radar-controlled guns because their touch was more delicate. They even took over the manning of the barrage balloons, huge, heavy monsters anchored to lorries.

The idea was for bombers to get tangled up in the guy ropes of the barrage balloons, although usually the bombers flew high to avoid them. The bombers also tried to defend themselves directly. Heinkels and Dorniers were fitted with a metal bar or wire which ran from a pole fitted to the nose to the tip of each wing, with a cutting edge to cut the ropes.

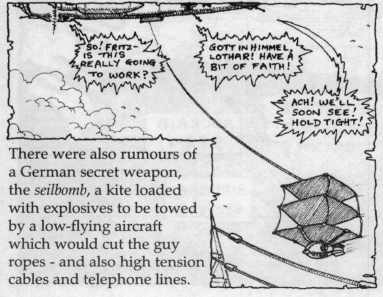

SO! FRITZ - IS THIS REALLY GOING TO WORK?

GOTT IN HIMMEL, LOTHAR! HAVE A BIT OF FAITH!

ACH! WE'LL SOON SEE! HOLD TIGHT!

There were also rumours of a German secret weapon, the *seilbomb*, a kite loaded with explosives to be towed by a low-flying aircraft which would cut the guy ropes - and also high tension cables and telephone lines.

Sometimes the balloons flew low and sometimes they flew high. There seemed to be no pattern to it. People used to remark on them, like the weather:

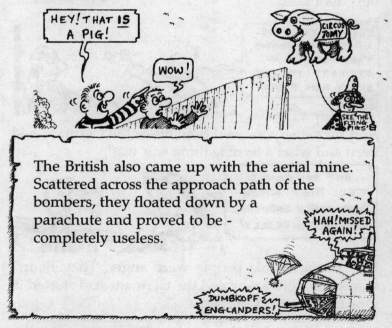

> I SEE THE BALLOONS ARE LOW TONIGHT!

> BUMP!

> BUMP!

> HMM!

As the writer Vera Brittain put it, the balloons looked like:

> ... *huge, oxidized fish or swollen pigs with large distended ears.*

> HEY! THAT **IS** A PIG!

> WOW!

> CIRCUS POMY

> SEE THE FLYING PIGS!

The British also came up with the aerial mine. Scattered across the approach path of the bombers, they floated down by a parachute and proved to be - completely useless.

> HAH! MISSED AGAIN!

> DUMBKOPF ENGLANDERS!

GOTCHA!

When the bombing started, not everyone took cover, far from it. A boy from Tyneside described the man next door jumping up and down on his bomb shelter and shouting encouragement at the gunners - as if they could hear him!

GET YOUR EYES CHARRED YE STUPID FOOLS! WHAT YE THINK YER PAID FOR?

And when the gunners missed, the whole district groaned like it was at a football match and the man next door said:

THEY WERE BRAVE LADS FOR GERMANS. THEY FLEW IN A STRAIGHT LINE AND DIDN'T RUN AWAY!

And then everyone said how brave the Germans had been and what a terrible thing war was!

...BUT YOU COULD TELL THEY WERE THOROUGHLY ENJOYING THEMSELVES REALLY!

But on the whole people were angry. They hadn't wanted to fight a war and the Germans had started it. One London girl's grandma:

..KEPT AN OLD SWORD IN THE CORNER THAT SOMEONE HAD GIVEN HER. SHE WAS GOING TO SLASH ANY GERMAN THAT CAME IN!

WOW!

FIRE!

At night, most of the bombers got through the defences and the scale of the inferno could be horrific. On one night, 16 April 1941 between 9pm and 5am, *150,000 fire bombs* and *800 tons of high explosive* were dropped on London. There was no let up. From 7 September 1940, there were raids for *seventy-six nights* in a row, bar one when it was foggy.

The Blitz became a way of life. Even as the bombs fell, the emergency services swung into action. Volunteer street fire parties were ready with stirrup pumps, and boys careered through the blazing streets on bicycles carrying messages about the sites worst hit. Professional firemen raced to give help.

It was exhausting work and the firemen were incredibly brave. Their eyes would puff up and go red from the showers of sparks. When bomb splinters struck a gas holder in Stratford, east London, firemen climbed up and stuck wet clay on the punctures to put out the fire before the gas holder exploded.

And when it was over, the firemen were often so exhausted that they fell asleep in their clothes even though they were stinking, soaked through with water from their hoses and coated in ash like ghosts.

ST. PAUL'S FAILS TO FALL

All through the Blitz a special band of 'friends' patrolled the dome and roof of St. Paul's Cathedral in the City of London. Altogether 800 fire bombs struck it, but all except one were thrown clear or fizzled out, and the one bomb which penetrated the dome caused some damage but nothing too serious. During the worst raids when all around was a blazing inferno the cathedral stood firm, a signal of hope to all Londoners, if a little alarming at times:

The Cathedral was above the capital as ever, except that it was red hot.

WELL – IT'S STILL THERE!

GOOD OLD ST. PAUL'S!

WOW – IT'S HOT!

RESCUE – IF YOU'RE LUCKY!

Immediately after a bomb fell, you could hardly see for dust, but as soon as possible voluntary rescue squads struggled to pull the victims from their bombed out homes. The heavy rescue squad was made up of men from the building trade. They had some of the worst jobs. One young man from London described the aftermath of a bomb:

The terrace had fallen like a pack of cards ... floors had to be jacked up and holes made through each ... I found a young woman crouching over her child. Both were dead though the child was still warm ...

Later in the war when the Blitz had started up again, another young rescuer described how soldiers came with large baskets in which they placed the remains of bits of girls from a bus queue. If they found no survivors, rescuers put up a flag to show that an area had been searched and there was no point in searching further.

The destruction was unpredictable. Shock waves from bombs have their own sinister rules of behaviour. Blast might knock down one house and leave a vase of flowers untouched on the window-sill next door. There were tales of people being stripped naked or sucked up chimneys.

To make sure that everyone was properly prepared, there was an ARP warden (stands for 'Air Raid Precautions'), usually part-time, for roughly every five hundred people. ARP wardens had a sand-bagged post for shelter but most of them preferred to be out on patrol. Like many others, they preferred the excitement of action to lying low.

THE MORNING AFTER

Immediately after a raid the homeless, caked in dried blood and covered in plaster from ceilings and walls, often with their faces and hands pitted with tiny splinters of glass, sought shelter where they could find it. Oddly, they could seem almost cheerful. This was because, if they weren't too badly injured, there was usually only one thing they cared about: their house might have been blown to bits and everything inside it destroyed - but was the family safe? If the family was safe, nothing else really mattered.

It was amazing how quickly things got back to 'normal', if you could call it normal. Within hours the injured had been carted off to hospital and the survivors had found shelter. By next morning, milk would be delivered through streets strewn with broken glass and carpeted in flattened bullets 'like little silver mushrooms'. In fact, the milkman was often the first with news of last night's destruction. Power and telephone lines were restored as soon as possible, not that many people had phones in those days.

Meanwhile, families and their pets were reunited at Incident Inquiry Points. And the WVS (Women's Voluntary Services) dished out tea and soup at emergency canteens, a vital service. The WVS had been started in 1938 by Lady Reading and was made up of about a million women, all unpaid and usually middle-aged. Because so many of them were respectable, middle-aged ladies, some people saw them as Lady Bossy rather than Lady Bountiful, but that was unfair. They were incredibly useful.

TAKE SHELTER!

The sensible thing was to take shelter during a raid, if you weren't a member of the Civil Defence or emergency services. Trenches were dug in public squares and there were shelters in the basements of large buildings. The children's hospital at Great

Ormond Street had an air raid shelter deep underground. As soon as the sirens sounded the nurses carried or hurried the children down from the wards.

The government built brick street shelters which were unpopular and almost useless. People preferred their Anderson shelters . You dug a hole in the back garden, a council lorry dumped fourteen sheets of corrugated steel in front of the house and you assembled it yourself over the hole at the back. Then you piled earth on top. Good for growing vegetables as well as keeping out the blast. When it was complete, a man from the council came round to check that you'd put it up right.

Later in the war, Herbert Morrison, the Minister of Home Security, introduced the Morrison Shelter, a large metal cage with a steel roof which you could

Designed by Dr. David Anderson, production and distribution organised by the Home Secretary, Sir John Anderson.

erect in any downstairs room which was large enough. It could withstand the collapse of a two storey building above your head and it saved many lives. The main problem was waking up in the morning: you banged your head if you forgot where you were.

DOWN THE TUBE

At the height of the Blitz in London, around 18,000 people per night chose to sleep on the platforms of the underground stations, far enough underground to be safe even from direct hits in most cases. Stations soon had their regulars but if you hadn't sorted out a regular spot you might have to travel from station to station searching for a space to lie down in. A white line about a metre from the edge allowed space for getting on and off the trains while people were settling down for the night.

Tube shelters were horribly uncomfortable. The deep ones had no toilets because there were no drains beneath for toilets to drain into. Some very bedraggled looking people would emerge in the morning to rush off home (if it was still there) for a wash and a bite of breakfast before work, or whatever else the day might hold for them.

BUSINESS AS USUAL

(SORT OF ...)

IT COULD HAVE BEEN WORSE

Britain soaked up the punishment and London, which took the brunt of the Blitz, kept going, in Churchill's words:

... like some huge prehistoric animal.

Like an animal, every morning while the Blitz went on, London picked itself up, shook itself down and went on living. Every weekday morning, Londoners boarded the crowded buses and tube trains - there were few cars and no petrol for them anyway. Then they picked their way through the rubble from the bus stop or tube station to their shops and offices. Shops always opened unless they'd been totally destroyed, and other businesses did likewise. Signs in the windows of bombed shops read:

'Shattered but not shuttered' was a good one. During

many raids, more people were injured by flying glass than directly by bombs. There were few large panes of window glass left in the country and there was no point in replacing large sheets of glass anyway, since they were bound to get shattered soon enough. Shops fixed up small display windows as soon as they could and boarded up the surrounding areas.

Business as usual was an exaggeration. At John Wadsworth's City Bank:

The branch moved back to working conditions of a century earlier. All entries were made by candlelight ... no telephones were working ... the customers of the branch suffered scarcely any inconvenience.

Business all right, but not as usual!

TOGETHERNESS

It's fair to say that the whole country had decided not to give in to despair. The Blitz brought out the best in people. Neighbours who hadn't spoken to each other for years passed cups of tea over the garden fence once the bombs began to fall. Even class divisions became slightly less important. The famous writer George Orwell put it like this:

England is a land of snobbery and privilege, ruled largely by the old and silly. But one has got to take into account the tendency of nearly all its inhabitants to feel alike and act together in moments of supreme crisis.

Early in the Blitz the bombs had fallen on the working class areas in the East End of London. The East Enders felt that nobody cared about them. King George VI and his queen were booed when they visited.

Luckily for national unity, Buckingham Palace was then hit three times and the Germans started to bomb the rich West End of London as well. And the king,

who could have done his work in the comfort of one of his other palaces outside London, stayed in Buckingham Palace specially to be bombed. After that, the East Enders welcomed him whenever he put in an appearance.

HAVING FUN

The truth is that quite a lot of people actually enjoyed the Blitz, at least if their loved ones were safe.

Churchill, for instance, unlike Hitler, loved the smell of explosives and talking to the men and women who manned the guns. This is how one young London girl described her feelings:

'I've been bombed,' I kept saying to myself. It seems such a terrible thing to say, but never in my life have I experienced such pure and flawless happiness.

Life was lived to the full. Why not - when you might not be alive tomorrow? Ballroom dancing was all the rage. It was so popular that people practised in their tea breaks and in their kitchens, they even practised in the parks although the grass must have made dancing difficult. At night there were plenty of nightspots tucked away in basements. It added spice to think that the person you were dancing with might not be alive for long. And the rich still had money to spend. The dance floor in the basement of the Dorchester hotel could pack in a thousand wealthy revellers.

There was no television and the cinema only cost nine old pence (less than five modern pence) - not a lot even then. So if dancing and drinking weren't your thing, you could always visit the cinema or the theatre. People would queue for hours for the cinema and many of them went every night of the week. There might be free tea and biscuits in the interval, and when

the sirens went off, the manager would walk onto the stage to tell people they could come back later.

If you didn't like dancing and you didn't want to go to the cinema, well, air-raid shelters were dingy and boring. Many people preferred the pubs, which often stayed open half the night, the piano tinkling and everyone singing to cover up the sound of the bombs outside. Hitler claimed that the British had taken to drink, to which the well-loved writer and radio broadcaster J.B. Priestley replied:

We had - long before the Nazis.

NOT SO GAY PAREE

In many ways people had a better time in London in the Blitz than they did in Paris without it. Paris was never bombed but Paris was under Nazi occupation. Even German servicemen had to behave themselves. They weren't allowed to dance or to smoke in the streets or in buses and on the metro, and they were forbidden to walk arm-in-arm with members of the opposite sex. NCOs (non-commissioned officers) had to be in by eleven and officers by midnight. All this was meant to make the Germans less unpopular with the French - but it didn't.

Skool - but not as usual

Most city schools had moved their children to the countryside during the great evacuation of 1939. The trouble was that by the time the Blitz started, many children had drifted home again. This meant that school in the big cities, especially in London, was a rather makeshift affair, often just half days in private houses. Lessons kept being interrupted by the air raid sirens - or by bombs. Then the children would queue up and head for the shelter with their teachers:

... the children just stood in absolute silence, and then moved in single file to the shelter, smartly and without running. They knew speed and order were of the essence.

During the hours in the shelters, the teachers got on with lessons as best they could and tried to keep their pupils from getting bored. Unfortunately, there was a lot going on outside which wasn't boring at all. When school was over or the 'all clear' sounded, children explored the bomb craters and ruined houses and collected shrapnel, fragments of exploded bombs. And some collected more dangerous items. One boy in Northampton managed to drag a machine gun out of a crashed bomber. He was seen in the school showers banging it on the floor so as to fire a bullet which had jammed in the breech. Not an activity to be recommended.

Another boy kept part of an airman's jawbone from the same plane as a souvenir. Also not an activity to be recommended.

PLUCKY BRITISH PULL THROUGH AGAIN

– AND AGAIN

Everyone was desperate to know what was happening in the war. Since there was no television, the wireless, as radio was then called, was a lifeline and everybody listened to it. People were more openly patriotic ◄ then than they are now. They had reason to be since their country was in danger of destruction. It was fairly common to stand up when the National Anthem was played on the BBC news, even if you were in the privacy of your own home.

 A *patriot* is someone who loves their country, in other words: they're *patriotic*.

Even while the bombs fell, when the news was over, battered atlases were taken down from dusty bookshelves and carefully studied. Although the British army had been driven out of France, British forces were still fighting in the Far East, in Africa and in the Mediterranean, and the Russians were fighting in the east. It was a world war after all. Everyone was an expert on military matters. Children argued about who were the best generals just as some of them argue about who are the best footballers nowadays.

Being wartime, the news was very carefully controlled by the government. Nothing was said which might discourage people or lead them to think that there was any chance that Britain might not win. Instead, the government encouraged the idea of the plucky British who kept cheerful through the horrors of the Blitz - and people lived up to the idea. It was the truth - even though it wasn't the *whole* truth.

Haw Haw!

Meanwhile, German radio did its best to persuade the British that they were really losing and they might as well give up. The Germans chose as their presenter William Joyce, an Irish American who read their English-language radio broadcasts in a strong upper-class accent. He was nicknamed 'Lord Haw Haw' because of the accent (try laughing in a posh way). Lord Haw Haw always started his broadcasts:

Germany calling!

Every day he told the British how badly they were doing and, at the start of the war, six million people listened to his broadcasts regularly. Later, when the BBC became a little more honest about how things were going, they stopped tuning into Haw Haw in such numbers. He took to drink towards the end and was executed in London for treason in 1945, when the war was over.

Don't you know there's a war on?

To keep people's spirits up, the BBC also broadcast several wonderful comedians. Jack Warner was a favourite with his list of absurd jobs, such as - putting the seeds in raspberry jam.

Jack Warner

But everyone's favourite was Tommy Handley, Mayor of Foaming-at-the-Mouth, a small (imaginary) seaside resort, creator of the 'Office of Twerps', and star of ITMA - It's That Man Again! His comic characters included the charlady Mrs Mopp.

ONE CARROT OR TWO?

RATIONS AND FASHIONS

FOOD FOR THOUGHT

The Blitz may have stopped in May 1941 before the German invasion of Russia, but the war went on. Having tried and failed to bomb Britain into submission, Hitler kept on with his other weapon - starvation. Before the war, Britain imported 60% of its food from other countries. If the Germans could cut off supplies of food, Britain would have to ask the Germans for peace on German terms. Other materials from overseas such as metal and oil were also vital to the war effort.

Most of Britain's supplies came from America, ferried across the Atlantic Ocean in huge convoys of up to a hundred merchant ships at a time. The convoys were protected by Royal Navy warships but German submarines, or 'U-boats ⟨ ' picked off the merchant ships one by one. In early 1941 when the Blitz was at its height, three British merchant ships were being sunk per day - and food was already in short supply in Britain. The *Battle of the Atlantic*, as it's known, was every bit as important as the Battle of Britain. It was a long, terrifying ordeal for the seamen who had to man

---

U-boat stands for *Unterseeboot* - 'undersea ship'.

the merchant ships, knowing that U-boats might strike at any time from the dark depths beneath. The British warships only just managed to save enough of the merchant ships to keep Britain supplied.

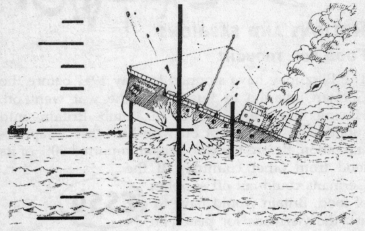

SCRAPING THROUGH

Owing to Hitler
Your fish will be littler.

As a result of the Battle of the Atlantic, food rationing was started in January 1940. Rationing meant that everyone was entitled to a certain quantity of basic foods - and no more. You weren't allowed to hog them. Without rationing, prices would have gone through the roof as supplies of food grew scarcer - the poor would have starved while the rich got fatter. At first only butter, sugar and bacon were rationed, but other foods soon followed. The rations weren't exactly generous. When rationing was at its worst there was only one egg per person per fortnight and 1 ounce (28.35 grams) of cheese per week. So while the bombs rained down outside, people treated themselves to 'delicacies' such as spam , a pink, tasteless processed meat, or 'bread and scrape' washed down with acorn coffee:

You scraped the butter on, then you scraped it off again.

Meanwhile, the government issued a steady stream of advice to housewives - in those days women did all the cooking. They were advised how to boil nettles:

Once thoroughly wet they lose the power of stinging.

And carrots were recommended as a sweetener, to be added to puddings and cakes.

To make sure that people didn't waste supplies of sugar, it was forbidden:

... to put any sugar on the exterior of a cake after the same has been baked.

If you had the money it was surprisingly easy to eat out, and that way you saved your ration coupons. You

Spam was generally thought to stand for 'Supply Pressed American Meat' although actually it was probably short for 'Spiced Ham'.

picked your way through the rubble to a 'British Restaurant'. There were several in all the major cities, run by local councils. They sold good food at a shilling a meal (5 pence in modern money). Fish, game and vegetables were never rationed anyway and there might be whale meat on the menu:

It tasted strongly of fish, unless you soaked it for twenty-four hours in vinegar - after which it tasted of vinegar.

As well as the cheap British restaurants there were some very smart restaurants in the West End of London which also stayed open for 'business as usual'. But if 'business as usual' meant dining on pheasant washed down with champagne while your fellow citizens took the brunt of the bombing and went without - well, it ceased to be popular. From 1942, no restaurant was allowed to charge more than five shillings a meal (25 pence in modern money).

THERE'S A SPIV IN MY GARDEN

Wherever food could be grown it *was* grown. London and other major cities sprouted thousands of allotments among the bomb craters and burned-out buildings. School playgrounds, traffic islands, front gardens, bomb craters and burned-out buildings - all were dug up and planted with vegetables. Even the moat round the Tower of London was used to grow peas and beans.

If the worst came to the worst, which it did all the time, and you weren't too careful about being legal, there was always the 'black market' - you could buy extra rationed food on top of your legal ration. In fact it was quite normal for people to finish their shopping by asking the shopkeeper if he or she had 'AUC' - 'Anything Under the Counter'. Failing that, most markets had a 'spiv' or two, as criminals were known. Spivs sold black market produce, usually either bought illegally from shopkeepers or else stolen.

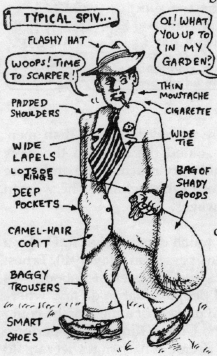

Shopkeepers had real power. Everyone had to be nice to the butcher if they wanted a decent cut of meat. Or if they were really lucky, they might know someone who was a farmer, which was even better. Farmers hardly ever went short of food. A Liverpool girl described how her farmer uncle used to kill a pig on the sly and give it to her father.

They used to put the dead pig in the bath, to soak overnight. My aunty went to the toilet in the night and she saw the pig lying in the blood-stained water. She let out a scream.

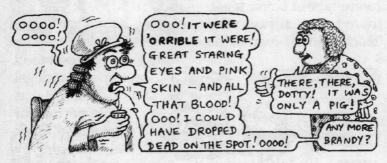

WOMEN'S WORK

Women often had more money to spend than men. Most of the men had joined the army or the navy where they weren't paid very much. More and more women took their places in the factories. The women started to earn proper wages.

Not that they had that much choice about it. Under a special act of Parliament passed in May 1940, Ernest Bevin, 'Ernie' for short, the Minister of Labour, was given the power to tell people what to do and where to go. In fact he had the powers of a dictator, he could 'direct any person in the United Kingdom to perform any service', he could decide what wages were paid and he could make strikes illegal. Bevin was from a very poor background and had started out as a farm labourer when he was only eleven. He used his powers to help poor working people as well as directing them for the war effort.

To begin with, Bevin hoped that women would work in the factories voluntarily, but they didn't, at least not many of them. Some were working already of course but those who weren't working were mostly very busy looking after their families. And some of them just didn't want to work anyway.

Britain desperately needed to keep the factories going full blast to supply the guns and other weapons needed to stop the Germans. That was why at the end of 1941 Bevin decided to conscript women, in other words - they would *have* to work whether they wanted to or not. They had a choice of sorts - between joining one of the women's services , the civil defence or

---

The women's services consisted of the ATS (Auxiliary Territorial Service), the WRNS or Wrens (Women's Royal Naval Service) and the WAAF (Women's Auxiliary Airforce).

industry. Thanks to Bevin, by 1943 nearly 90% of unmarried women and 80% of married women were doing some kind of war work. Britain was the only country in the world where this happened in such numbers. In Germany there was no conscription of women at all until 1943.

Most women chose to work in industry and only a quarter chose the women's services. This was because most of them didn't like the idea of being shouted at by sergeants or having to wear uniforms. And at the start of the war, the women's services simply weren't set up for women. Apart from anything else, no woman was going to use a toilet without a door such as the men had to use.

The work the women had to do was hard. In Woolwich Arsenal, which churned out weapons and was a major target for bombers at the height of the Blitz, the workers, men and women, worked twelve hours a day, seven-day and seven-night weeks alternatively. But at least the women made £10.00 per week with danger money if they worked in a danger area, for instance putting the caps on detonators. That was good money in those days.

Not that women were paid equally with men. They had to fight for equal pay and they didn't always get it by any means. One of their few advantages was the tea break which they were entitled to under the factory acts of the nineteenth century, passed

to protect women and children from the worst effects of the Industrial Revolution. Men had to fight for the right to have tea breaks - which was hardly the same as fighting for equal pay.

TIME FOR TURBANS

Because women were now working at 'men's' jobs, they needed to wear suitable clothes. That often meant trousers, still quite shocking on women in those days. And because it was important that their long hair didn't fall into dangerous machinery, it also meant *turbans*. The turban became a major fashion item until the end of the war.

Unfortunately, the fashionable look for women was heavily made up - red lips, lots of face powder and plenty of mascara - and there wasn't any make-up, or not much anyway. Women had to make do as best they could. Here are some tips for a 1940s fashion victim:

Melt down the stubs of old lipsticks and mould new ones from the old.

Use beetroot juice when your lipstick's completely run out.

Use soot from the chimney for mascara, or burnt cork.

Tear up an old parachute for silk underwear.

Smear gravy browning on your legs to look like stockings, then paint a 'seam' down the back - just hope it doesn't rain.

No time for turn-ups

Hitler also managed to ruin men's fashions during the war. Scarcity of cloth meant that it was almost impossible to look anything other than shabby and down-at-heel:

I hope you don't want to read the newspaper!

Most things were in short supply, not just food, make-up and material for clothes. 'Waste not want not' was the order of the day. The government asked people to take fewer baths so as to save energy, and to run their baths to a maximum depth of 5 inches (12.7 cm, it's not much - check it out). Hotels painted a 'Plimsoll line' round the inside of their baths to show the proper depth for guests to run the water to.

As for paper, teachers would get cross with their pupils if they filled up their exercise books too quickly! Many schools went back to using chalk and slates because paper was in such short supply. And even the poshest homes provided torn up squares of newspaper in the toilet instead of toilet paper. Toilet paper was a thing of the past.

BLITZ BRAINBOGGLER

TEST YOUR KNOWLEDGE OF LIFE ON THE
HOME FRONT WITH THIS BARMY QUIZ...

1. WHY ARE CARROTS SWEET?

   a) PEOPLE DIP THEM IN SUGAR.
   b) THEY HAVE A LOT OF SUGAR IN THEM.
   c) THEY'RE NICE TO OTHER VEGETABLES.

2. WHY WILL FISH BE LITTLER?

   a) THEY WON'T REALLY — THERE'LL JUST BE FEWER OF THEM.
   b) HITLER'S BOFFINS HAVE INVENTED A SHRINK-RAY.
   c) THEY'RE ON A DIET.

3. WHAT DOES A.T.S. STAND FOR?

   a) ARMY TEA SET.
   b) AUXILIARY TERRITORIAL SERVICE.
   c) ALBERT TRENCH'S SOCKS.

ANSWERS: 1: (b). 2: (a). 3: (b).

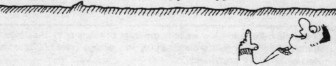

WHISTLE WHILE YOU WORK

Britain is not known for its aluminium mines. In fact it doesn't have any. It used to have lots of tin, gold, iron and lead mines long ago, but most of them were mined out centuries before World War II started. Metal was desperately needed for tanks, aircraft and other armaments. Aluminium from saucepans, silver paper and milk bottle tops was melted down to build Spitfires. Iron was melted down for tanks and guns . Ernie Bevin encouraged children to collect metal. Here's a song they may have sung while they went about it:

 Even today, there are low walls at the front of many older buildings with stumps of iron railings still sticking out. The railings were cut down to be used as scrap for armaments.

BOMBED OUT!

BOMBING THE BOMBERS

TO BOMB - OR NOT TO BOMB? THAT IS THE QUESTION

Thousands dead, countless businesses and houses destroyed, no turn-ups on trousers - a lot of reasons for revenge bombing on the Germans. But in 1941 most people (German as well as British) still thought it was wrong to bomb civilian targets - and it's mostly civilians who get killed when you bomb a city. In fact, at the start of the Blitz, German bombers had orders to return to base without dropping their bombs if they couldn't see their targets clearly enough to be sure of bombing them.

LOOK! THEY'RE TURNING BACK!

MUST BE THE CLOUD COVER! THEY CAN'T SEE A TARGET!

WELL PLAYED! JOLLY DECENT OF OLD JERRY!

Night bombing made a nonsense of all that. One thing you can't do at night is to see your target clearly. But even in April 1941 when German night bombing had killed thousands of civilians, only 50% of British people thought that the revenge bombing of German civilian targets was acceptable; 40% still disapproved.

Interestingly, it was the people in the East End of London and in other big cities, who had suffered worst, who were least keen on revenge bombing.

Despite public opinion, the big-wigs of the RAF always believed that massive bombing of German cities, 'strategic bombing' as it was called, was worth it because it would break the will of the German people and thus help win the war. An odd idea, given that all the evidence pointed the other way - and that the evidence lay before their eyes in Britain itself:

The more you bomb people, the more obstinate they become.

Why would the Germans be any different?

In the winter of 1940, before the Blitz was even over, Hugh Dowding and Keith Park were both sacked. Dowding was eventually replaced by Trafford Leigh-Mallory, who had always disagreed with Dowding's defensive tactics during the Battle of Britain and had campaigned long and hard against him. When the Air Ministry published a booklet *The Battle of Britain* shortly after, neither Dowding nor Park got so much as a mention.

Once the men who had master-minded the defence of Britain had been removed, and so shabbily, and the threat of immediate invasion was over, the RAF went full steam ahead for a massive bombing campaign against Germany. They had just the right man for the job: Arthur 'Bomber' Harris, soon to be head of Bomber Command. Aircraft factories began to churn out more heavy, long range bombers.

YOU BOMBED US, NOW WE'LL BOMB YOU

As soon as they came off the production line, Bomber Harris put his bombers to work.

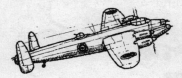 

February 1941: Stirlings, the first British four-engined bombers attack Rotterdam in German-occupied Holland.

15 November 1941: four-engined Lancaster bombers delivered to front line squadrons in Britain.

23 February 1942: Bomber Harris becomes Air Officer Commander-in-Chief of Bomber Command.

28 March 1942: British bombers set fire to the medieval centre of Lübeck. Harris picks Lübeck, because with its lovely wooden buildings it is: 'built more like a firelighter than a human habitation'. He wants to show that 'saturation bombing ' can destroy an entire city.

23 April 1942: Furious at the attack on Lübeck, Hitler orders reprisal raids on beautiful British towns. This is the beginning of the 'Baedeker' raids, named after a well-known tourist guide. Historic cities such as York, Exeter and Bath are bombed.

IRISH SEA

NORTH SEA

YORK

ATLANTIC OCEAN

BATH

EXETER

THE BAEDEKER RAIDS

ENGLISH CHANNEL

30 May 1942: Harris launches the first 'thousand bomber' raid. In one and a half hours, 1,500 tons of bombs are dropped on the ancient city of Cologne, utterly destroying the centre with great loss of life to the civilian population. This is followed by two further such raids, on Essen on 1 June, and on Bremen on 25 June.

Saturation bombing meant dropping so many bombs in such a short space of time that a city's fire and other rescue services would be unable to cope.

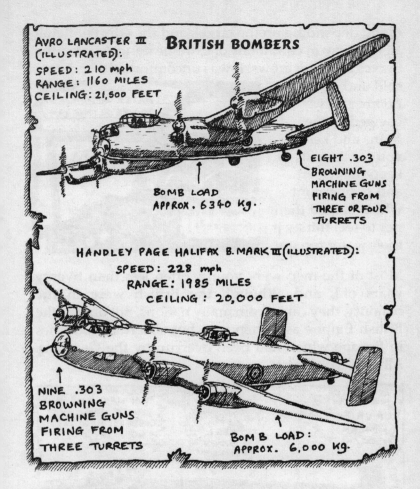

AVRO LANCASTER III
(ILLUSTRATED):
SPEED: 210 mph
RANGE: 1160 MILES
CEILING: 21,500 FEET

BRITISH BOMBERS

BOMB LOAD
APPROX. 6340 kg.

EIGHT .303
BROWNING
MACHINE GUNS
FIRING FROM
THREE OR FOUR
TURRETS

HANDLEY PAGE HALIFAX B. MARK III (ILLUSTRATED):
SPEED: 228 mph
RANGE: 1985 MILES
CEILING: 20,000 FEET

NINE .303
BROWNING
MACHINE GUNS
FIRING FROM
THREE TURRETS

BOMB LOAD:
APPROX. 6,000 kg.

BEAN THERE, COME BACK

The flight across the English Channel and then across night-time Europe to targets deep inside Germany was long (roughly a thousand miles to Berlin) and incredibly dangerous. The men who undertook it were incredibly brave. In 1942, 1,400 British bombers were shot down over Germany and 2,700 were damaged. The journey there and back could take most of the night, depending on the target, and the effort of flying all that way in conditions of extreme danger tested the nerves of the air crews. It was uncomfortable, and very cold and noisy. Bomber crews chewed coffee beans and keep-you-awake pills to keep them alert, and peppermint which helped them not to feel thirsty if their water ran out.

Most of the men were young, often less than twenty years old, and although the British were in the majority, they came from many nations, not only of the British Empire as it then was, but also from countries in Europe which had been overrun by the Germans. All were volunteers.

FLYING REFRIGERATORS

America entered World War II in December 1941, after

Germany's Japanese allies had bombed the American fleet at Pearl Harbor, Hawaii, in the Pacific. From that moment, the writing was on the wall for Hitler - if only he'd been able to read it.

It was very simple. American factories could churn out as many fighters and bombers as they wanted to, and they were too far away for the Germans to be able to bomb them. On the other hand, the British and Americans could keep on bombing German factories from bases in Britain. There could only be one result: the British and Americans would end up with a lot more planes than the Germans and the Germans would lose the war. The German high command chose to ignore this rather obvious fact. Goering indeed claimed that the Americans:

... can make cars and refrigerators but not aircraft.

An odd thing to say about the country which invented powered flight.

The first squadrons of the United States Air Force arrived in Britain in June 1942. To start with their numbers were small and they had a lot to learn about flying in war conditions. Even by February 1943, the RAF flew so many more raids that they could lose more aircraft on an average night than the Americans lost in the entire month. But the Americans built up their strength. Their tactics were to fly very high and to bomb by daylight. Unfortunately, the higher you go, the colder it gets. This was especially dangerous in the

bitter winter of 1942-43. Frostbite was a routine danger for young American pilots at the beginning. Some froze and died of suffocation while in the air.

AND FLYING FORTRESSES

American bombers were heavily armed, some were called 'flying fortresses'. The theory was that by flying their heavily armed bombers at high altitude they would minimise the risk to their pilots. They flew in a carefully worked out 'box' formation.

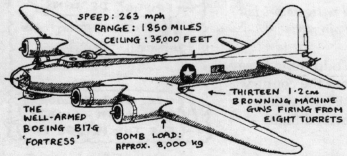

Any German fighter attacking such a formation had to fly through a web of overlapping fire from the American machine guns. To counteract the threat of the American box and the threat from the RAF, the Germans began to fly in *Wilde Sau* ('Wild Sow') units, which flew by sight only - and by the seat of their extremely brave pants. Their most successful tactic against the American 'box' was the mass head-on attack. The German pilots would fly straight at the incoming bombers at hair-raising speeds of up to 965 kph (600 mph).

BOMB LOAD : APROX. 8,000 kg

B-24J LIBERATOR (ILLUSTRATED) :
SPEED : 278 mph
RANGE : 1700 MILES
CEILING : 28,000 FEET

↑ TEN 1·2 cm BROWNING MACHINE GUNS FIRING FROM FIVE TURRETS

ROUND-THE-CLOCK SHOCKS

The Ruhr region was the industrial heartland of Germany and where the giant arms manufacturer Krupp had its main factories. In 1939 Goering had jokingly told a German audience:

> *If an enemy bomber reaches the Ruhr, my name is not Hermann Goering. You can call me Meier* .

5 March 1943: a massive RAF raid on the Krupps works at Essen in the Ruhr valley, starting the battle of the Ruhr.

April 1943: Germans start to make jokes about a character called 'Stupid Meier'.

Meier is a very ordinary German surname, a bit like 'Smith' in England.

25 July 1943: the first major allied attack on Hamburg, given the code name 'Gomorrah' (after a city in the Bible which was destroyed by God) by Bomber Harris. British bombers strike at night and the attack is continued by American flying fortresses the following day - the first overwhelming use of 'round-the-clock bombing'.

28 July 1943: a second major raid on Hamburg. In the firestorm which follows, temperatures at the centre of the city rise to over 1000°c. The intense heat sucks air into the centre, rooting up entire trees in the process. The charred bodies of adults shrink to the size of children, and the bodies of children to the size of large dolls. When the attacks on Hamburg finish on 2 August, a million people have fled the area and 40,000 are dead. Any pretence by British Bomber Command of not bombing civilian targets has been forgotten.

WINDOW

Hamburg was the first time the RAF used 'window', 92 million bits of it, over the city. 'Window' was strips of aluminium foil cut to a length which confused enemy radar defences. Dumped from the incoming bombers, 'window' completely confused the German radar-directed anti-aircraft guns and fighter planes. It was a major reason why Hamburg suffered so terribly.

AN EXAMPLE TO US ALL

By the time the bombs rained down on Hamburg a majority of British people had come to regard the bombing of German cities as a necessary evil, but not everyone. After Hamburg some started to change their minds. George Bell, bishop of Chichester remarked:

... this progressive devastation of cities is threatening the roots of civilisation.

And, although Hamburg was a human catastrophe, it didn't stop the war. Despite the bombing, German factories kept churning out weapons as before. The German government encouraged German civilians to copy the bravery of their British enemies during the bombing of London two years earlier.

On the plus side, the bombing forced the German high command to recall German fighters from Russia to defend German skies. This helped the Russians who had been under attack since Operation Barbarossa in May 1941. 'Stupid Meier' had to do something to protect his people.

DOODLE- BUGS AND BEYOND

OH NO, NOT AGAIN!
BABY BLITZ

Britain was like an aircraft carrier, moored to the side of German-occupied Europe. From her deck, planes could bomb Germany - and troops could prepare for the invasion and liberation of Europe.

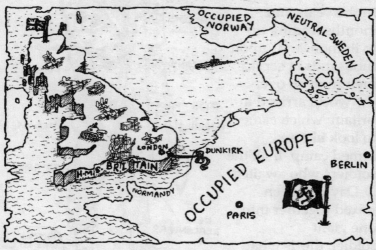

Not that the aircraft carrier was safe. In December 1943, Hitler ordered a further bombing campaign against Britain. The 'Baby Blitz', as it became known, was in revenge for Hamburg and for the bombing of Berlin which took place from November 1943 until March 1944. This attack on Berlin was the biggest bombing campaign of the war.

The Baby Blitz wasn't as bad as the Blitz of 1940-41, but bad enough. 1,556 were killed, mainly around London. It started a fresh evacuation of Londoners into the countryside.

GIANT ISSUES

The Allied invasion of Europe was planned for 6 June 1944, code name D-Day. In the years and months leading up to it, thousands upon thousands of service men from all over the world arrived in Britain, which came to look like an armed camp. If all the soldiers who awaited D-Day had been mixed together into one giant soldier, this is what he might have looked like:

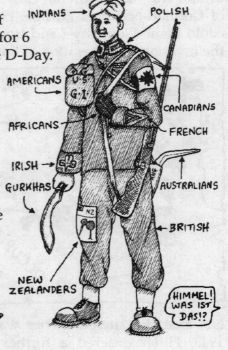

Americans made up the largest contingent after the British. They were known as 'GIs' because the words 'Government Issue' were stamped on their uniforms. The GIs made a big impression. During the horrors of the Blitz and the drab days of rationing that continued after, British people had watched endless American movies. The movies cheered them up and reminded them that there was another comfortable, normal life to be lived once the war was over.

Now here were the Americans - in Britain.

They seemed just like film stars. We were so drab. It was another world.

American soldiers were paid three times as much as British soldiers and their uniforms looked better. They were generous, they would give gifts of nylon stockings and cigarettes to their British girlfriends, and chewing gum to the children when the children asked:

Got any gum, chum?

British men, who'd done most of the fighting and suffering up till then, weren't very happy that these rich, handsome foreigners should be so popular with their girls, but there was nothing much they could do about it - especially since the Americans had come over to help them win the war. Many British children discovered that they had a new American or Canadian 'uncle' while their fathers were off fighting.

WHITE, BLACK AND BLUE

One thing that did surprise the British about the Americans was how racist they were. Black Americans were kept in separate black regiments and black and white never mixed. The British were far from perfect about other races, but nothing like this. A woman in Cirencester described how she organised a dance and invited the GIs who were stationed nearby. An officer said that they would love to come but black and white couldn't come together because there would be a fight. She was furious and said:

D-DAY

Before dawn had fully broken on 6 June 1944, the skies above southern Britain were darkened by countless

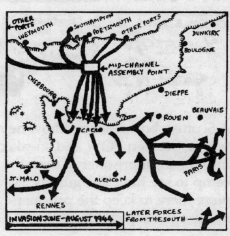

bombers on their way to bomb the German defences in Normandy and the earth shook with the roar of their engines. Below them, the roads to the ports on England's south coast were clogged with thousands of lorries carrying troops and their weapons. Already in the dark of the night many regiments had boarded their transport ships and set sail across the Channel for the beaches of Normandy. D-Day had come as planned, the largest water-born invasion that the world has ever seen.

The invasion was long, slow and bloody and the Germans fought back like tigers, but gradually the massive power of the allied forces ground them down. Allied armies swept through occupied France to Paris.

POW!

As the Allies began to win the war in Europe, a new foreign invasion of Britain began - trainloads of German prisoners of war, or 'POWs'. They joined German and Italian POWs already in Britain from the campaigns in Africa and Italy. Most of these POWs weren't Nazis and a lot of them were simply glad to have got out of the war alive. They were employed on farms and other places where they could be useful. In sleepy country villages the POWs often made life more interesting. A boy in Cheshire described how two German POWs helped his father's lorry business. His mother used to give them dinner. One of them had been a lion tamer before the war:

The Italian POWs were very popular in local choirs because of their tenor voices.

A Scottish boy described how he made friends with a German POW and sneaked into the local prisoner of war camp to see him. The guards were there to keep the prisoners in - not to keep children out:

They were so glad to see children ... They made toys for us, model boats and tanks, really beautiful.

V IS FOR VERY UNPLEASANT

On 13 June, a week after D-Day, a large object crashed into the ground in Kent, one of ten launched from across the Channel by the Germans. This was the first *Vergeltungswaffe I*, 'Vengeance Weapon No.1' or V1 flying bomb, commonly called the doodle-bug, to hit British soil. The doodle-bug was Hitler's secret

weapon, his next-but-last throw of the dice before final defeat. Britain was about to experience the last bombing campaign of the war.

Doodle-bugs flew at 640 kph (400 mph) and carried a load of 8,500 kg of high explosive. Compared to human-piloted bombers they were stupid. They flew in a straight line and a lot of them were shot down. Skilled RAF pilots could fly alongside and tip the doodle-bug over with a wing. However, enough got through to wreak havoc. The V1 raids weren't as bad as the main Blitz, because they didn't start so many fires, but they were a lot worse than the Baby Blitz.

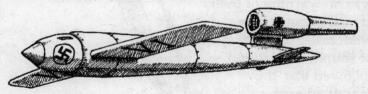

The engine of a V1 sounded like a very noisy lawn mower, but it was when the engine cut out that you had to worry. That was when the doodle-bug plunged towards earth:

> *It seemed to take ages and it was the most helpless feeling I know. At the bottom of the dive there were people waiting to die.*

Even General Eisenhower, the Allied Supreme Commander, used to mutter 'Keep going, keep going' when one flew over.

Worse was to follow. Hitler had another secret weapon up his sleeve, his last - but not his least. V2 flying bombs were nearly 13 metres long, they carried a tonne of high explosives and with their rocket engines they reached maximum speeds of 5,800 kph (3,600 mph). Launched from launch pads deep in German-occupied Holland, they climbed up to eighty kilometres (50 miles) into the sky before curving down and finally, plunging vertically to earth at 3,200 kph (2,000 mph). There was no warning of their arrival because they went faster than the speed of sound, their sound followed like 'the roar of an express train'. Nothing could shoot them down.

The main V campaign lasted until late August 1944, when the allied troops overran the launch pads in northern France. During that time 10,500 doodle-bugs were launched and 5,475 people were killed. They caused a third mass evacuation from London. Some children went back to the houses they had first stayed in at the beginning of the war.

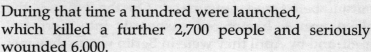

Meanwhile, there was only one way to stop the V2s and that was to capture their launch pads, which took another six months. During that time a hundred were launched, which killed a further 2,700 people and seriously wounded 6,000.

DRESDEN

The last V2 fell on 27 March 1945, but in the meantime one last, terrible tragedy was about to be played out. On 13 February 1945, pursuing Bomber Harris's attempt to 'break the will' of the German people, allied bombers attacked the ancient city of Dresden. Dresden was not a military target, there were no factories worth speaking of in the town. In the fire storm which the bombs created, Dresden was destroyed and more people were killed than in all the German raids on Britain put together.

BRAVE NEW WORLD

THEY THINK IT'S ALL OVER ...

THE END

By the time Dresden was destroyed, allied bombers had the run of the skies over Germany. German fighters fought back as best they could, but they were outnumbered and outgunned. On the ground, the allied armies hammered eastwards into Germany itself, and by April they were in Berlin where they met the Russians who had invaded Germany from the east. The war was over. On 29 April 1945, in his bomb-proof shelter beneath the heart of the city, Hitler married his long-time mistress Eva Braun and the next day the two of them committed suicide.

STREET PARTIES

It has been calculated that throughout the previous five years, the air raid sirens had gone off every thirty-six hours on average. 48,000 Londoners had been killed by German bombs, and a total of 60,595 civilians had been killed in the country as a whole. On top of that, the RAF had lost 520 airmen during the Battle of Britain and 47,268 during the bombing of Germany. Many more had died fighting in the army and navy. Now it was time to celebrate that the horrors were past. On 8 May, a week after Hitler had committed suicide, Britain celebrated Victory in Europe Day, 'VE Day' for short. The lid was at last taken off the pressure cooker, and the tension and fear of six years of war was about to be sung, drunk and danced out in one vast sigh of relief. In preparation for the party, bomb sites were raided for timber. Then when the celebrations began, bonfires were lit on almost every street in London. In fact there were so many fires that it looked like the Blitz had started all over again.

Every street had its street party. The houses were decked with Union Jacks. A little girl from Liverpool described how:

My Aunty Al got her piano out and played in the street and everyone was singing and dancing. The party went on all through the night.

BACK TO NORMAL

When the party was over, it was time to get back to normal. During the next few months, five million men came back from the navy and the armies in Europe and other parts of the world, to a Britain which some of them hadn't seen since the war began. It was sometimes a strange homecoming. There were husbands and wives who hadn't seen each other for more than five years, five years of suffering, excitement and danger. To the children, their father was often a complete stranger. A girl from Cambridge described how she'd avoided this. Throughout the war she had:

... a terrible fear that when my father came home I wouldn't recognise him. I kept a photograph of him by my bed, and every night I studied it closely, kissing it goodnight, and put it to bed in a cardboard box with a blanket.

Meanwhile the GIs and other foreign troops started to pack up and go home. 60,000 British 'GI brides' went with them back to America - all those presents of nylon stockings hadn't been wasted.

Women began to leave their jobs in the factories. At that time they were expected to go back to looking after their families and it's probably fair to say that most of them wanted to.

... if he can get a regular job, I won't go to work. I'll stay at home and have children.

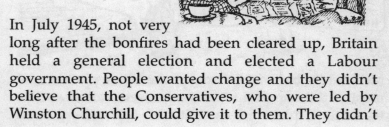

AND LABOUR PARTIES

So Britain was on its way back to being boring and normal again. But most people were determined that although it might go back to being boring it would not go back to being the unfair and unequal place that it was before the war started. In 1939 at the start of the war, shocked by the poverty of evacuee children from London, a woman had written a letter to *The Times* newspaper saying:

The evacuation has caused us to lift the stone and see what is crawling around underneath. Let's make a promise that at the end of the war we won't just put the stone back.

In July 1945, not very long after the bonfires had been cleared up, Britain held a general election and elected a Labour government. People wanted change and they didn't believe that the Conservatives, who were led by Winston Churchill, could give it to them. They didn't

want to put the stone back on all the poverty and inequality.

There were so many things to do. So much had been destroyed. The 1945 Labour government turned out to be one of the great reforming governments of the twentieth century, and many of their reforms are still with us today. They started a crash programme of house building, improved welfare payments for people in need, gave the opportunity of good secondary education for all - and started the National Health Service.

Meanwhile back in Germany, the allies put on trial most of the important Nazis who were still alive. The trials took place in the city of Nuremberg, and

Hermann Goering was the most senior Nazi there. He looked confused. Perhaps it was the drugs, or perhaps he just couldn't believe that the Nazi dream was over. On 15 October 1946, a few hours before he was due to be executed, he took poison and killed himself.

HOW DID IT ALL GO WRONG?.. WHERE IS YOUR 1000-YEAR REICH NOW, MEIN FÜHRER?.. CALL ME MEIER!.. HAH! HAH!..

Goering was a Nazi, but if you'd asked him he would have said that he was first and foremost a German nationalist who loved his country. It was the extreme nationalism of people like Goering which had started the trouble in the first place. The Nazis had whipped the German people into a frenzy of hatred for others. That didn't happen in Britain. A miner's daughter described the difference in attitude:

... things like nationalism and patriotism don't need to be taught or encouraged, because people's natural fear when an emergency arises will make them come together.

The bravery and patriotism of the British people during the Blitz are proof that she was right.

TARGET PRACTICE!

You're training to be an ack-ack gunner. Aim too wide of the mark, whether high or low, and you'll fail the test. Fortunately, for this test your targets are not real bombers!

1. How many tons of high explosive were dropped on Britain during the Blitz?

1,000,000
25,300
27,500

2. How many allied soldiers escaped from Dunkirk?

338,000
568,000
768,000

3. How many German barges would be needed for Operation Sealion?

8,000
10,000
3,000

4. How many funeral forms were printed in Britain before the start of the war?

800,000
300,000
1,000,000

5. How many men had joined the Home Guard by August 1940?

2,000,000
1,000,000
1,500,000

6. How many British bombers were shot down over Germany in 1942?

3,800
1,400
4,800

7. How many died during the raids on Hamburg between 25 July and 2 August 1943?

40,000
200,000
15,000

8. What temperature was reached at the heart of the firestorm in Hamburg on 28 July 1943?

600°c
800°c
1,000°c

9. What was the maximum speed of a V2 rocket bomb?

1,000 kph
4,800 kph
5,800 kph

10. How many British civilians were killed by German bombs during the war?

60,000
60,595
55,955

Answers

1. - 27,500 tons (page 6) 2. - 338,000 (page 21)
3. - 3,000 (page 23) 4. - 1,000,000 (page 24)
5. - 1,000,000 (page 31) 6. - 1,400 (page 99)
7. - 40,000 (page 104) 8. - 1,000°c (page 104)
9. - 5,800 kph (page 114) 10. - 60,595 (page 117)

INDEX

QUOTATIONS

For quotations on pages 25,26,28,62,65,73,84,94,112 & 117: I am grateful to *The Children of the Blitz* by Robert Westall, published by Viking in 1985. This is an excellent book and well worth reading if you can find a copy in your local library or bookshop.

For the quotations on pages 27,29,32,62,75,110,118 & 119: I am grateful to *Don't You Know There's a War On?* by Jonathan Croall, published by Hutchinson in 1988. Another excellent book.

For the quotations on pages 61,64,71,72,109,113 & 119: I am grateful to *A People's War* by Peter Lewis, published by Thames Methuen in 1984. This book contains vivid first-hand accounts by wartime survivors.

The quotation about snobbery on page 72 is from the *Lion and the Unicorn* by George Orwell (Copyright © George Orwell 1941) reproduced by permission of A M Heath & Co. Ltd. on behalf of Bill Hamilton as the Literary Executor of the Estate of the late Sonia Brownell Orwell and Martin Secker & Warburg Ltd.

My sincere thanks for all quotations contained in this book.

ABOUT THE AUTHOR

Bob Fowke is a popular author of children's information books. Writing under various pen names and with various friends and colleagues, he has created many unusual and entertaining works on all manner of subjects.

There's always more to his books than meets the eye - look at all the entries in the index of this one!

What They Don't Tell You About ...
ORDER FORM

0 340 70921 9	ANGLO SAXONS	£3.99
0 340 71330 5	ART	£3.99
0 340 78806 2	CHARLES I AND THE CIVIL WAR	£3.99
0 340 78807 0	THE COLD WAR	£3.99
0 340 65613 1	ELIZABETH I	£3.99
0 340 85182 1	THE GUNPOWDER PLOT	£4.99
0 340 63621 1	HENRY VIII	£3.99
0 340 69349 5	LIVING THINGS	£3.99
0 340 73611 9	OLYMPICS	£3.99
0 340 71329 1	PLANET EARTH	£3.99
0 340 63622 X	QUEEN VICTORIA	£3.99
0 340 70922 7	ROMANS	£3.99
0 340 67093 2	SHAKESPEARE	£3.99
0 340 68995 1	STORY OF MUSIC	£3.99
0 340 69350 9	STORY OF SCIENCE	£3.99
0 340 78805 4	WORLD WAR I	£3.99
0 340 68612 X	WORLD WAR II	£3.99

All Hodder Children's books are available at your local bookshop or newsagent, or can be ordered direct from the publisher. Just write to the address below. Prices and availability subject to change without notice.

Hodder Children's Books, Cash Sales Department, Bookpoint, 130 Milton Park, Abingdon, Oxon, OX14 4SB, UK.
Email address: orders@bookpoint.co.uk

Please enclose a cheque or postal order made payable to Bookpoint Ltd to the value of the cover price and allow the following for postage and packing:
UK & BFPO - £1.00 for the first book, 50p for the second book, and 30p for each additional book ordered, up to a maximum charge of £3.00. OVERSEAS & EIRE - £2.00 for the first book, £1.00 for the second book, and 50p for each additional book.

If you have a credit card you may order by telephone - (01235) 400414 (lines open 9am-6pm, Monday to Saturday; 24 hour message answering service). Alternatively you can send a fax on 01235 400454.